Salads

igloo

Published by Igloo Books Ltd
Cottage Farm
Sywell
NN6 0BJ
www.igloo-books.com

10 9 8 7 6 5 4 3 2 1

ISBN: 978 1 84852 728 7

Project Managed by R&R Publications Marketing Pty Ltd

Food Photography: R&R Photostudio (www.rrphotostudio.com.au)
Recipe Development: R&R Test Kitchen

Front cover photograph © Getty Images/Caren Alpert

Printed in and manufactured in China

Contents

Asparagus and Baby Green Beans with Hazelnut Dressing

Preparation 20 mins **Cooking** 5 mins **Calories** 284

Dressing
3 tbsp lemon juice
3 tbsp white wine vinegar
3 egg yolks
1 cup hazelnut oil (or any other nut oil)
½ small bunch dill, chopped
1 cup chopped toasted hazelnuts

Salad
6 bunches asparagus, trimmed
1kg (2¼ lb) baby green beans, topped and tailed
2 red capsicums, finely julienned

1 To make the dressing, combine the lemon juice, vinegar and egg yolks in a blender and blend until pale and creamy. Slowly drizzle in the oil until the dressing comes together. Stir in the chopped dill and toasted nuts and season to taste.

2 Bring a large saucepan of water to the boil, add the asparagus and beans and simmer for approximately 1–2 minutes until the vegetables are just tender.

3 Drain and toss with the dressing, nuts and finely sliced capsicum and serve on the same day.

Serves 8–10 as an entrée

Summer Salad of Grilled Chicken, Spinach and Mango

Preparation 1 hr 30 mins **Cooking** 2 hrs 20 mins **Calories** 90

Salad

6 tomatoes
10 basil leaves, sliced
10 mint leaves, sliced
salt and pepper
½ tsp sugar
12 small chicken fillets (from breasts)
1 bunch asparagus
1 avocado
1 bunch scallions
8 firm button mushrooms
2 firm mangoes
3 handfuls baby spinach leaves
½ cup toasted hazelnuts, lightly crushed
½ cup toasted brazil nuts, lightly crushed
½ cup toasted pistachios, lightly crushed

Dressing

2 tsps honey
2 tbsps balsamic vinegar
3 tbsps raspberry vinegar
2 tbsps soy sauce
2 tsps Dijon mustard
2cm (1in) piece ginger, crushed
2 cloves garlic, crushed
1 tsp chili paste
2 tbsps lemon juice
2 tbsps olive oil
salt and freshly ground black pepper

1 Preheat the oven to 160°C (325°F). Slice the tomatoes in half lengthways, and top with sliced basil, mint, salt, pepper and sugar. Bake for 2 hours.

2 In a large jug, beat together all the dressing ingredients until emulsified (thickened).

3 Marinate the chicken in ½ cup of dressing, reserving the remainder for later. Allow the chicken to marinate for 1 hour minimum (or up to 4 hours). Heat a non-stick skillet pan and cook the chicken fillets over a high heat until cooked through, 2–3 minutes on each side. Transfer the cooked fillets to a plate and keep warm.

4 Steam the asparagus until tender then refresh under cold water. Halve the avocado, peel, and dice the flesh. Slice the scallions diagonally and thinly slice the mushrooms. Dice the mango flesh.

6 To make the salad, place the well-washed spinach leaves in a large bowl and add the blanched asparagus, sliced scallions, mushrooms and roasted tomatoes, cut into quarters. Add the reserved dressing and toss thoroughly.

7 Divide the salad evenly among individual plates and add some mango and avocado cubes. Top with 2 fillets of chicken, and a generous sprinkling of nut medley. Serve immediately.

Serves 6

Watercress and Pear Salad

Preparation 15 mins **Cooking** None **Calories** 134 **Fat** 8g

2 bunches watercress, picked and washed
3 tbsps olive oil
1 tbsp lemon juice
½ tbsp white wine vinegar
salt and pepper
3 pears, finely sliced
shavings of Parmesan

1 Wash and dry the watercress well.

2 Beat the olive oil, lemon juice and white wine vinegar with salt and pepper until the mixture has thickened slightly.

3 Slice pears finely and combine with watercress in a bowl.

4 Drizzle over dressing just enough to coat the leaves. Place on a platter and top with shavings of Parmesan.

Serves 6–8

Note: You can use wild arugula instead of watercress.

Fijian Kokoda

Preparation 4 hrs 15 mins **Cooking** None **Calories** 568

1½ kg (3½lb) firm white fish
1 cup fresh lime juice (or lemon juice)
300ml (11fl oz) canned coconut milk
salt and pepper
1 small red capsicum, finely diced
1 small green capsicum, finely diced
1 small red chili, ground
1 firm tomato, finely diced
lime or lemon wedges

1 Cut the fish into 1cm (½in) cubes and mix with 200ml (7fl oz) of the lime juice, half the coconut milk, salt and pepper to taste. Stir well and marinate for 4 hours.

2 When the fish is firm and looks opaque (cooked), drain away and discard the liquid.

3 Mix the drained fish with the capsicum pieces, chili and tomato. Add the remaining coconut milk and lime juice and stir to combine thoroughly.

4 Serve cold in glasses with wedges of lime or lemon as an entrée.

Serves 4

Note: Kokoda is a traditional dish from Fiji where it is prepared using a local fish called mahi-mahi.

Asian Gingered Coleslaw

Preparation 30 mins **Cooking** None **Calories** 155

½ large curly cabbage, very finely shredded, about 5 cups

4 baby bok choi, leaves separated and minced

8 scallions, julienned lengthways

200g (7oz) canned sliced water chestnuts, drained

2 medium carrots, finely julienned

2 stalks lemongrass, finely sliced

4 kaffir lime leaves, finely sliced

Dressing

2 tbsps mayonnaise

2 tbsps yogurt

juice of 2 lemons

juice of 1 lime

4cm piece ginger, shredded

4 tbsps rice vinegar

salt and pepper

Garnish

1 bunch cilantro, roughly chopped

½ cup toasted peanuts or sunflower seeds

1 Mix the cabbage in a large bowl with the sliced bok choi, scallions, water chestnuts, carrots and finely sliced lemongrass and lime leaves. Toss thoroughly.

2 In a jug, beat together all the dressing ingredients until smooth and well seasoned then pour over the salad ingredients and toss thoroughly until all the vegetables are coated with the dressing.

3 To serve, mix through the cilantro at the last minute and sprinkle with the crushed peanuts or sunflower seeds.

Serves 6

Japanese Rice Noodle Salad

Preparation 20 mins **Cooking** 15 mins **Calories** 537

250g (9oz) long, flat rice noodles

1 tsp olive oil

2cm (1in) piece ginger, shredded

1–2 small fresh red chilies, deseeded and minced

1 red capsicum, cut into small chunks

6 scallions, sliced on the diagonal

½ bunch cilantro

juice of 1 lime

1 tbsp Japanese rice vinegar

1 tbsp soy sauce

2 tbsps vegetable stock

3 tbsps sesame seeds

1 Fill a large jug or bowl with hand-hot water and immerse the rice noodles, allowing them to soak until soft, about 5–10 minutes. Drain and rinse under cold water to refresh them, then place the noodles in a large mixing bowl.

2 Heat the olive oil in a small non-stick skillet and add the ginger and chilies and sauté gently for a minute or two. Add the chopped capsicum pieces and raise the heat to medium-high and stir-fry the capsicum pieces until they are softened. Add the scallion slices and continue to cook for a further 2 minutes.

3 Tip the capsicum mixture into the mixing bowl with the noodles and add the cilantro, tossing thoroughly.

4 In a small jug, beat together the lime juice, rice vinegar, soy and stock and toss through the noodles. Sprinkle with the sesame seeds and chill before serving.

Serves 2

Marinated Salmon, Cucumber and Daikon Salad

Preparation 2 hrs **Cooking** None **Calories** 226

700g (1½lb) fillet of salmon,
6 tbsps mirin (sweet Japanese rice wine)
3 tbsps Japanese soy sauce
4cm (2in) piece ginger, shredded
1 tsp toasted sesame oil
1 cucumber
1 tsp sea salt
1 tbsp caster sugar
3 tbsps rice vinegar
curly endive, well washed and dried
1 daikon (daikon), finely julienned

1 Ask your fishmonger to slice the salmon thinly as for smoked salmon. If they can't or won't, have the skin removed and slice the salmon into very thin strips – if you feel you are able to slice the salmon on an angle this would be desirable, but if not, cut straight down.

2 Beat the mirin, soy, ginger and sesame oil together then remove 2 tbsps and reserve. Pour the remainder into a shallow bowl and add the sliced salmon fillet, allowing the fish to marinate for 2 hours.

3 Meanwhile, peel the cucumber and using a vegetable peeler or food slicer, cut the cucumber into long, thin slices and place these in a bowl. Mix together the sea salt, sugar and rice vinegar and drizzle over the cucumber, tossing well to coat the slices in the dressing.

4 Arrange slices of marinated salmon on the plates then place the curly endive and daikon in the centre. Weave some drained cucumber slices through the salad then drizzle a little of the reserved mirin dressing over the salad.

Serves 6

Marinated Bean Salad

Preparation 4–6 hrs **Cooking** 15 mins **Calories** 303

100g (4oz) green beans, cut in half

2 small zucchini, cut into matchsticks

1 small carrot, cut into matchsticks

250g (9oz) canned kidney beans, drained and rinsed

250g (9oz) canned chickpeas, drained and rinsed

250g (9oz) canned lima beans, drained and rinsed

1 small red capsicum, cut into strips

¼ cup fresh parsley, chopped

¼ cup fresh basil, chopped

Dressing

3 tbsp olive oil

1½ tbsps red wine vinegar

1 clove garlic, crushed

freshly ground black pepper

1 Steam the green beans, zucchini and carrot until just tender. Drain and refresh under cold running water.

2 To make the dressing, place oil, vinegar, garlic and black pepper to taste in a screw-top jar and shake well to combine.

3 Place cooked vegetables, kidney beans, chickpeas, lima beans, capsicum, parsley and basil in a large salad bowl. Spoon over dressing and toss to combine. Cover and refrigerate for 4–6 hours. Just prior to serving, toss again.

Serves 4

Note: Canned beans are a quick and nutritious alternative to dried beans. There is some loss of B vitamins during canning, but not a lot. A couple of cans of beans in your cupboard are always a handy standby for an easy, no-fuss, high-fiber meal.

Tuscan Tomato and Bean Salad

Preparation 35 mins **Cooking** None **Calories** 410

12 sun-dried tomatoes, drained

⅓ cup rice vinegar

1 tbsp olive oil

2 tsps molasses

1 tbsp soy sauce

salt and pepper

150g (5oz) baby arugula leaves

150g (5oz) watercress

8 tomatoes, diced

6 scallions, sliced

80g (3oz) Kalamata olives, stones removed

800g (1¾lb) canned cannellini beans, rinsed and drained

100g (4oz) chopped toasted walnuts

1 Combine 1 cup boiling water and drained sun-dried tomatoes and allow to stand until the water cools. Add the rice vinegar, oil, molasses and soy sauce and purée in a blender until smooth. Add salt and pepper.

2 Thoroughly wash the arugula and watercress until no trace of grit remains. Place the freshly washed leaves in a large mixing bowl and add the diced tomatoes, scallions, olives and cannellini beans.

3 Pour over the sun-dried tomato dressing and toss well to coat all the leaves. Serve immediately garnished with the toasted walnuts.

Serves 4

Warm Salad of Capsicum and Rosemary

Preparation 10 mins **Cooking** 40 mins **Calories** 127

6 large capsicums of assorted colors

2 tbsps virgin olive oil

1 large red onion, peeled and cut into eights

3 tbsps fresh rosemary

3 cloves garlic, crushed

1 tbsp balsamic vinegar

salt and freshly ground pepper

1 Slice the 4 sides off each capsicum and discard the seed core. Slice the capsicum pieces into long, thin strips.

2 Heat the olive oil in a skillet and add the onion and rosemary and sauté on a high heat for 3 minutes. Add the garlic and all the capsicum pieces and toss thoroughly with the rosemary-flavored oil.

3 Continue cooking over a low heat for 30 minutes, stirring often, until the capsicum pieces are wilted and the onion has caramelised a little. Add the balsamic vinegar and cook for a further 5 minutes.

4 Add salt and pepper to taste and serve warm.

Serves 4

Note: To turn this salad into a true antipasto, cook the capsicum/onion mixture over a medium–high heat (instead of low heat) for 30 minutes until the capsicum pieces are almost meltingly soft.

Calabrian Salad

Preparation 1 hr 15 mins **Cooking** 20 mins **Calories** 218

4 fist-sized potatoes, scrubbed and washed, not peeled

8 firm tomatoes

3 red onions, peeled and sliced thinly, then soaked in cold water for 30 minutes

15 small, whole, fresh basil leaves

1 heaped tsp dried oregano

4 tbsps olive oil

3 tbsps white or red wine vinegar

salt and pepper

1 Cover the potatoes in cold water and boil until just tender all the way through, about 15–20 minutes. Drain and leave aside until just cool enough to handle, then peel and slice thinly.

2 Cut the tomatoes in half and remove the hard inner core. Slice the tomatoes and add them to the potatoes. Add the finely sliced red onions and toss well.

3 Add the basil leaves, oregano, olive oil, vinegar and a little salt and pepper. Toss everything carefully and serve at once.

Serves 6

Greek Orzo Salad with Olives and Capsicums

Preparation 30 mins **Cooking** 30 mins **Calories** 789

350g (12oz) orzo or rice-shaped pasta

180g (6oz) feta cheese, crumbled

1 red capsicum, finely chopped

1 yellow capsicum, finely chopped

1 green capsicum, finely chopped

180g (6oz) pitted Kalamata olives, chopped

4 scallions, sliced

2 tbsps drained capers

3 tbsps pine nuts, toasted

Dressing

juice and zest of 2 lemons

1 tbsp white wine vinegar

1 tbsp crushed garlic

1½ tsps dried oregano

1 tsp Dijon mustard

1 tsp ground cumin

5tbsp olive oil

1 Cook the orzo in a large pot of boiling salted water until tender but still firm to bite. Drain and rinse with cold water then place in a large bowl with a little olive oil from the dressing ingredients.

2 Add the crumbled feta cheese, chopped capsicums, Kalamata olives, scallions and capers.

3 To make the dressing, beat together the lemon juice and zest, vinegar, garlic, oregano, mustard and cumin in a small bowl. Gradually add the olive oil then season to taste with salt and pepper.

4 Drizzle the dressing over the salad and toss thoroughly then garnish with the toasted pine nuts.

Serves 4

Roasted Beets, Orange and Fennel Salad

Preparation 35 mins **Cooking** 1 hr **Calories** 418

5 large beets

1 tbsp brown sugar

1 tsp salt

2 tbsps chopped fresh rosemary

3 tbsps olive oil

1 bulb fennel

3 blood oranges

150g (5oz) toasted hazelnuts, crushed

Dressing

½ cup chopped dill

2 tbsps balsamic vinegar

½ cup olive oil

salt and pepper

1 Heat the oven to 180°C (350°F).

2 Wash and trim the beets at root and stem ends but do not peel.

3 In a small bowl, mix together the brown sugar, salt, rosemary and the 3 tbsps of olive oil until well blended then add the whole beets and toss in the oil mixture, making sure that the beets' skins are all shiny. Wrap each of the beets in aluminum foil and place in a baking dish then roast for approximately 1 hour or until just tender. Peel the beets and cut into thick slices.

4 Very finely slice the fennel bulb and peel the oranges, trimming any white pith. Cut the orange into segments.

5 Next, make the dressing. Combine the dill, balsamic vinegar, olive oil, salt and pepper to taste and beat well until thick.

6 Arrange the beets on a serving platter with the thinly sliced fennel and orange. Drizzle over the dill vinaigrette then scatter the crushed hazelnuts on top.

Serves 6–8

Salad of Sautéed Duck with Thyme and Honey

Preparation 25 mins **Cooking** 15–20 mins **Calories** 547

3 duck breasts, skin on
salt and pepper
1 tbsp vegetable oil
1 tbsp butter
1 sprig thyme, leaves picked from the stalk
2 tbsps honey
1 tbsp lemon juice
2 tbsps walnut oil
fine grey sea salt and freshly ground black pepper
200g (7oz) mixed baby lettuce leaves, washed and spun dry
6 large cherry tomatoes
basil leaves to garnish

1 Heat the oven to 190°C (380°F). Season the duck breasts with a little salt and pepper.

2 Heat the oil in a pan until almost smoking then add the duck breasts, skin-side down, and cook on a high heat until the skin is deep caramel brown. Transfer the pan containing the duck to the preheated oven until the duck is cooked rare, about 7–10 minutes. (Do not turn the duck breasts over.)

3 Remove the pan from the oven and remove the breasts from pan, keeping them warm, and drain and discard the excess fat. Add the butter and when it begins to bubble add the thyme leaves then the honey. When simmering, replace duck breasts, skin-side up.

4 Cook for a further minute on low heat then remove pan altogether.

5 Beat together the lemon juice, walnut oil, salt, pepper and the pan juices and mix well. Toss the lettuce leaves through a little of the dressing.

6 Divide the lettuce leaves between the plates, garnish with tomatoes. Slice the duck breasts and arrange around the salad, drizzling any excess honey sauce over the duck slices. Garnish with basil leaves and serve.

Serves 4

Tuscan Panzanella with Roasted Tomato Vinaigrette

Preparation 35 mins **Cooking** 10 mins **Calories** 401

300g (11oz) stale, rustic Italian-style bread (about ¼ loaf)

2 tbsps olive oil

1 tbsp fresh rosemary, chopped

500g (18oz) assorted tomatoes

1 cucumber

10 Kalamata olives

1 small red onion, finely chopped

10 basil leaves

2 mint leaves, finely sliced

½ tbsp fresh marjoram

Dressing

2 small tomatoes

¼ cup olive oil

1 tbsp red wine vinegar

½ tbsp balsamic vinegar

2 cloves garlic

salt and freshly ground pepper

1 Cut the bread into cubes and toss with 2 tbsps olive oil and the rosemary. Spread out on a baking tray and bake at 200°C (400°F) for 5 minutes until golden, then cool.

2 To make the dressing, heat a heavy pan and brush the skins of the small tomatoes with a little olive oil. Cook these whole tomatoes in the pan until well blackened all over. Purée with the remaining olive oil, vinegars, garlic, salt and pepper to taste. Set aside.

3 Remove the seeds from the other tomatoes and chop into small chunks. Peel the cucumber and remove the seeds by running a teaspoon along the central seed area. Slice finely. Remove the stones from the olives by squashing them with the wide blade of a knife.

4 In a mixing bowl, place the bread cubes, tomatoes, cucumber, onion, olives and torn basil leaves. Add the chopped mint and marjoram. Mix well. Pour the dressing over the salad and toss thoroughly. Allow to sit for 10 minutes then serve.

Serves 4

Warm Lima Bean and Prosciutto Salad with Arugula

Preparation 12 hrs **Cooking** 1 hr 10 mins **Calories** 221

500g (18oz) dried lima beans
2 tbsps olive oil
½ tsp dried chili flakes
3 cloves garlic, crushed
100g (4oz) prosciutto, roughly chopped
salt and freshly ground pepper
10 basil leaves, torn
2 handfuls arugula leaves

1 Place the lima beans in a large bowl of warm water and soak overnight.

2 The next day, drain the beans and place them in a saucepan of cold water. Bring to the boil and simmer for 1 hour or until just tender. Drain, reserving a ladle or two of the cooking water.

3 Heat the olive oil in a medium saucepan. Add the chili flakes and garlic and sauté briefly until the garlic is golden. Add the prosciutto and stir over moderate heat until beginning to brown, about 2 minutes. Add the lima beans and cook, tossing occasionally, until heated through, about 3 minutes, adding some of the reserved cooking water if the mixture seems a little dry.

4 Season with salt and pepper and add the torn basil leaves and arugula. Toss gently then serve warm.

Serves 4

Roasted Beets Salad with Balsamic and Dill

Preparation 30 mins **Cooking** 45 mins **Calories** 262

24 very small beets, greens attached if possible

1 tbsp olive oil

salt and freshly ground pepper

15g butter

2 tbsps balsamic vinegar

3 tbsps fresh dill, snipped

100g (4oz) hazelnuts, roasted and chopped

2 tbsps sour cream or yogurt (optional)

1 If your beets have their greens attached remove them and set aside. Wash the beets and scrub them until clean. Trim the bottom if necessary but be careful not to cut the beets themselves.

2 Toss the beets and olive oil together then place them in a baking dish. Cover with aluminum foil or a lid and roast at 200°C (400°) for 30–45 minutes or until tender.

3 Remove the beets from the oven and cool then peel the skin away and discard. Cut the beets in half lengthways and add salt and pepper to taste.

4 Meanwhile, wash the beets' greens thoroughly to remove all traces of sand and grit. Heat the butter in a sauté pan and add the greens, tossing for 1 minute until wilted. Remove the greens and add the balsamic vinegar and bring to the boil, beating with the butter. Return the peeled beets and toss them in the balsamic until it has reduced and leaves a shiny sheen on the beets.

5 Transfer the beets to a platter or bowl and arrange with the wilted beets leaves. Scatter over the dill and roasted hazelnuts, adding small spoonfuls of the sour cream or yogurt if desired. Add black pepper to taste.

Serves 6

Endive Salad with Apples, Blue Cheese and Pecans

Preparation 20 mins **Cooking** None **Calories** 448

5 heads endive

1 red apple

1 green apple

200g (7oz) young arugula leaves

1 cup coarsely chopped pecans, toasted

100g (4oz) crumbled blue cheese such as Gorgonzola

¼ cup olive oil

¼ cup walnut oil

¼ cup sherry wine vinegar

1 large shallot, ground

salt and pepper

1 Cut the endive in half lengthways then lay the endive cut-side down on a board and cut the leaves into thin strips.

2 Thinly slice the unpeeled apples and toss with the lemon juice.

3 Wash the arugula leaves and drain well.

4 Combine endive strips, apple slices, arugula, toasted pecans and blue cheese in a large bowl.

5 Beat the oils, vinegar and shallot in small bowl then season to taste with salt and pepper.

6 Drizzle the dressing over the salad and toss thoroughly. Serve immediately.

Serves 6

Caramelized Trout Salad with Cellophane Noodles

Preparation 35 mins **Cooking** 15 mins **Calories** 302

2 tbsps olive oil
10 shallots, chopped
200g (7oz) brown sugar
5 tbsp fish sauce
½ cup fresh ginger, julienned
10 small chilies, halved, seeds removed and julienned
2 tbsps lime juice
200g (7oz) cellophane noodles
1 bunch fresh cilantro leaves, chopped
500g (18oz) trout fillets, cut into 3cm (1in)-thick strips

1 Heat the olive oil and gently sauté the chopped shallots until golden. Add the sugar and heat in the pan until the sugar has dissolved. Cook on a medium heat until the mixture has caramelized, about 5 minutes, stir well. Add the fish sauce, ginger, chilies and lime juice and stir well until combined. Keep hot.

2 Soak the cellophane noodles in hot water until they have softened, about 10 minutes, then refresh in cold water. Drain then add the cilantro leaves and just enough brown sugar sauce to moisten the noodles.

3 Meanwhile, pan-fry or broil the fish fillets until just cooked.

4 Arrange the noodles on individual plates then place the fish pieces decoratively on the cellophane noodles. Garnish with extra chilies and cilantro leaves and spoon more sauce over.

Serves 4

Note: You could use tuna or salmon instead of trout as an alternative.

Asian Chicken Bok Choi Salad

Preparation 40 mins **Cooking** None **Calories** 673

8 fresh or dried shiitake mushrooms

10g (⅓oz) black cloud ear fungus

800g (1¾oz) cooked chicken, skin off, shredded

1kg (2¼lb) packet fresh Asian noodles

200g (7oz) fresh snowpeas, diagonally sliced

4 baby bok choi, well washed and leaves separated

1 red capsicum, diced

4 scallions, finely sliced

250g (9oz) canned sliced water chestnuts, drained

1 tbsp freshly ground ginger

¼ cup plain yogurt

3 tbsps soy sauce

1 tbsp hoisin sauce

3 tbsps mirin

3 tbsps rice vinegar

3 tbsps sweet chili sauce

1 tbsp fish sauce

juice of 1 lime

salt and pepper

2 tbsps slivered almonds, toasted

1 bunch of chervil, parsley or cilantro

1 If using dried shiitake, soak in hot water for 15 minutes then drain and slice. If using fresh shiitake, slice finely. Soak the black cloud ear fungus for 15 minutes then drain. Rinse the soaked mushrooms thoroughly in cold water.

2 Place the shredded cooked chicken in a large bowl. Pour boiling hot running water over the noodles until they have separated then shake off excess water and add to the chicken. Add the mushrooms, sliced snowpeas, baby bok choi leaves, diced capsicum, sliced scallions and water chestnuts and toss well.

3 In a jug, beat together the ginger, yogurt, sweet soy sauce, hoisin, mirin, rice vinegar, sweet chili, fish sauce, lime juice, salt and pepper to taste. Add to the chicken salad and toss very well until all the ingredients are coated. Garnish with the toasted slivered almonds and chopped chervil, parsley or cilantro and serve.

Serves 6–8

Note: Dried shiitake mushrooms and black cloud ear fungus are both available from Asian grocery stores.

Gingered Almond Broccoli Salad with Cellophane Noodles

Preparation 25 mins **Cooking** 6–8 mins **Calories** 247

Noodles

100g (4oz) dried cellophane noodles

2 tbsps fish sauce

2 tbsps rice vinegar

2 tbsps mirin

1 tsp brown sugar

½ cup fresh cilantro, chopped

Salad

1 tbsp peanut oil

1 tbsp shredded fresh ginger

1 small hot red chili, very finely sliced

4 cloves garlic, crushed

4 scallions, minced

500g (18oz) broccoli florets, trimmed

10 fresh shiitake mushrooms, sliced

200g (7oz) baby corn

3 tbsps soy sauce

3 tbsps mirin

2 tbsps rice vinegar

1 cos lettuce, shredded

100g (4oz) blanched almonds, toasted

1 First, prepare the noodles. Fill a deep jug or bowl with very warm water and soak the cellophane noodles for about 10 minutes or until they are soft and tender. Drain. Mix together the fish sauce, rice vinegar, mirin and sugar then toss through the cellophane noodles. Add the cilantro, mix well and set aside.

2 Heat the peanut oil in a wok and add the ginger, chili, garlic and scallions and toss thoroughly until the scallions have wilted, about 3 minutes.

3 Add the broccoli florets and toss well until bright green. Add the mushrooms and corn and continue tossing over a high heat. Add the soy, mirin and rice vinegar and continue cooking for 1 minute.

4 Add the noodles and mix well then remove the pan from the heat.

5 Divide the shredded lettuce among the plates then top with the broccoli noodle mixture. Garnish with toasted almonds and extra chopped cilantro.

Serves 6–8

Note: When you buy heads of broccoli, trim each little head of broccoli from the main stem – this is called a floret.

Gingered Thai Rice Salad

Preparation 20 mins **Cooking** 10 mins **Calories** 556

2 cups long-grain rice

5 scallions, finely chopped on the diagonal

3 medium carrots, coarsely shredded

4 baby bok choi, washed and chopped

2 kaffir lime leaves

½ cup cilantro, coarsely chopped

1½ cups chopped roasted peanuts

1 tbsp black sesame seeds

2 tbsps Thai basil, finely chopped

Dressing

2 tbsps peanut oil

juice of 2 limes

3 tbsps Thai fish sauce

2 tbsps ground sugar

2 tbsps sweet chili sauce

1 tbsp ground ginger

pinch of chili powder or cayenne pepper

salt and pepper

1 Bring a large pot of salted water to the boil then add the rice and simmer for 8–10 minutes or until tender. Drain and rinse thoroughly in cold water then drain again.

2 Meanwhile, make the dressing. Beat together the oil, lime juice, fish sauce, brown sugar, sweet chili sauce, ginger, chili powder, salt and pepper and allow to sit until the rice is ready.

3 Prepare all the vegetables then mix thoroughly with the finely sliced lime leaves, cilantro, chopped roasted peanuts and sesame seeds. Add the cooked rice and mix well.

4 Toss the rice and vegetable mixture with the dressing, tossing thoroughly to coat all the ingredients, then add the Thai basil and serve.

Serves 6

Cabbage and Chinese Noodle Salad

Preparation 10 mins **Cooking** 5 mins **Calories** 578

Salad
½ Chinese cabbage
4 baby bok choi
8 scallions
½ bunch fresh cilantro
¾ cup flaked almonds, toasted
½ cup pine nuts, toasted
100g (4oz) fried Chinese noodles

Dressing
4 tbsps peanut oil
2 tbsps balsamic vinegar
2 tbsps fresh lime or lemon juice
1 tbsp brown sugar
1 tbsp soy sauce
salt and cracked pepper

1 Finely shred the cabbage and transfer to a large mixing bowl. Thoroughly wash the bok choi then slice them crosswise and add to the cabbage.

2 Wash the scallions then slice finely on the diagonal, and add these to the cabbage mixture together with the washed and roughly chopped cilantro.

3 Under the broiler or in a dry skillet, toast the almonds and pine nuts and set aside to cool.

4 Mix the nuts and noodles with the cabbage salad.

5 To make the dressing, beat all the ingredients together with a beat until thick. Drizzle over the salad and toss thoroughly then serve immediately.

Serves 4

Summer Greens with Lime and Cilantro

Preparation 15 mins **Cooking** 8 mins **Calories** 296

250g (9oz) snowpeas, topped and tailed

2 bunches asparagus, cut in half

250g (9oz) sugar snap peas, topped and tailed

250g (9oz) fresh peas (shelled)

125g (4oz) cherry tomatoes, cut in half

Dressing

2 tbsps lime juice

3 tbsps cilantro, chopped

½ cup olive oil

1 tbsp white wine vinegar

1 Blanch the snowpeas, asparagus and sugar snap peas in boiling water for 30 seconds, drain and refresh in a bowl of iced cold water. Drain well.

2 Cook peas in boiling water for 2 minutes, or until tender then drain and refresh in iced water. Drain well. Combine all vegetables and cherry tomatoes.

3 For the dressing beat all ingredients until well combined and toss over vegetables and serve.

Serves 4–6

Note: Add 1 small red chili chopped and ½ cup diced mango to the dressing for added flavor.

Vietnamese Green Papaya Salad

Preparation 15 mins **Cooking** None **Calories** 65

Salad

750g (1¾lb) green papaya
4 scallions, very finely julienned
½ white radish (daikon), very finely julienned
12 leaves mint
12 leaves Thai basil
¼ bunch cilantro, leaves only
1 clove garlic, crushed
2 tbsps dried shrimp or crushed peanuts

Dressing

¼ tsp shrimp paste
3 tbsps rice vinegar
3 tbsps lime juice
2 tbsps fish sauce
2 tbsps sugar
1 tbsp sweet chili sauce

1 Finely julienne the papaya and toss with the finely julienned scallions, daikon, chopped fresh herbs and garlic.

2 To make the dressing, dilute the shrimp paste in 2 tbsps boiling water, then beat with all other dressing ingredients. If the sauce is a little too acidic, add a little extra water as required to dilute the flavor to your tastes. Continue beating until the dressing is well mixed.

3 Toss the dressing through the papaya/ vegetable mixture, taking care to disperse the dressing thoroughly. Scatter over the dried shrimp or peanuts to serve.

Serves 8

Thai Calamari Salad

Preparation 30 mins **Cooking** 10 mins **Calories** 143

3 calamari tubes, cleaned

185g (6oz) green beans, sliced lengthways

2 tomatoes, cut into wedges

1 small green pawpaw, peeled, deseeded and shredded

4 scallions, sliced

30g (1oz) fresh mint leaves

30g (1oz) fresh cilantro leaves

1 fresh red chili, chopped

Lime Dressing

2 tsps brown sugar

3 tbsps lime juice

1 tbsp fish sauce

1 Using a sharp knife, make a single cut down the length of each calamari tube and open out. Cut parallel lines down the length of the calamari, taking care not to cut right the way through the flesh. Make more cuts in the opposite direction to form a diamond pattern.

2 Heat a non-stick skillet over a high heat, add calamari and cook for 1–2 minutes each side or until tender. Remove from pan and cut into thin strips.

3 Place calamari, beans, tomatoes, pawpaw, scallions, mint, cilantro and chili in a serving bowl.

4 To make dressing, place sugar, lime juice and fish sauce in a screw-top jar and shake well. Drizzle over salad and toss to combine. Cover and stand for 20 minutes before serving.

Serves 4

Note: You could use 500g (18oz) of baby octopus instead of the calamari in this salad.

Caesar Salad

Preparation 15 mins **Cooking** 20 mins **Calories** 269

2 cloves garlic, crushed

6 tbsps olive oil

9 anchovy fillets

juice 1½ lemons

good dash of Worcestershire sauce

dash of mustard

1–2 tbsps white wine vinegar

4 eggs, boiled for 1 minute (yolks only)

2 thick slices country bread

salt and pepper

100g (4oz) prosciutto

3 heads Romaine or cos lettuce

40g (1½oz) shredded Parmesan cheese

freshly ground pepper

1   Preheat the oven to 220°C.

2   In a large mixing bowl, place the garlic and 4 tbsps olive oil and, using the base of a metal spoon, squash and pound the garlic into the oil. Add the anchovies and mash these into the oil mixture. Beat in the lemon juice then Worcestershire sauce, mustard and white wine vinegar, mixing thoroughly to incorporate each ingredient before the next is added.

3   Crack the eggs carefully after they have been boiled for 1 minute then discard the whites and add the yolks to the mixing bowl. Mix these in thoroughly, incorporating them into the other ingredients. Set aside.

4   Cut the bread into cubes and toss with the remaining olive oil, salt and pepper. Transfer to a baking tray and bake the cubes until golden, about 15 minutes. Cool.

5   Crisp the prosciutto in a skillet then break into smaller pieces.

6   Place the well-washed lettuce leaves in a mixing bowl and toss them thoroughly in the dressing for several minutes until all the leaves have been coated. Add the bread cubes, Parmesan cheese, and finish with black pepper and crisp prosciutto. Serve immediately.

Serves 6

Warm Potato Salad

Preparation 8 mins **Cooking** 15 mins **Calories** 93

500g (18oz) baby new potatoes

Mustard Dressing
2 tbsps wholegrain mustard
2 tbsps fresh parsley, chopped
2 tsps chopped capers
1 clove garlic, crushed
1 tbsp lemon juice
freshly ground black pepper

1 Cook potatoes in boiling water until just tender. Drain well and place in a heatproof bowl.

2 To make dressing, place mustard, parsley, capers, garlic, lemon juice and black pepper to taste in a bowl and mix to combine. Spoon dressing over hot potatoes and toss to combine. Serve immediately.

Serves 4

Note: 150g (5oz) of chopped grilled bacon could be added to the salad when spooning over the dressing.

Seared Scallop Salad

Preparation 10 mins **Cooking** 6–8 mins **Calories** 813

2 tsps oil
2 cloves garlic, crushed
375g (13oz) scallops, cleaned
4 slices bacon, chopped
1 cos lettuce, leaves separated
60g (2oz) croutons
20g (1oz) Parmesan cheese

Mustard Dressing
3 tbsps mayonnaise
1 tbsp olive oil
1 tsp sesame oil
1 tbsp vinegar
2 tsps Dijon mustard

1 To make dressing, place mayonnaise, olive oil, sesame oil, vinegar and mustard in a bowl, mix to combine and set aside.

2 Heat oil in a skillet over a high heat, add garlic and scallops and cook, stirring, for 1 minute or until scallops just turn opaque. Remove scallop mixture from pan and set aside. Add bacon to pan and cook, stirring, for 4 minutes or until crisp. Remove bacon from pan and drain on absorbent paper.

3 Place lettuce leaves in a large salad bowl, add dressing and toss to coat. Add bacon, croutons and shavings of Parmesan cheese and toss to combine. Spoon scallop mixture over salad and serve.

Serves 2

Salmon and Lentil Salad

Preparation 15 mins **Cooking** 5 mins **Calories** 606

1 cos lettuce, leaves separated and torn into large pieces

200g (7oz) green lentils, cooked and drained

200g (7oz) red lentils, cooked and drained

250g (9oz) cherry tomatoes, halved

150g (5oz) wholemeal croutons

1 tbsp chili oil or vegetable oil

375g (13oz) salmon fillets, skin removed, cut into 3cm wide strips

20g (1oz) Parmesan cheese

freshly ground black pepper

Dressing
½ cup mayonnaise

2 tbsps vegetable stock

1 tbsp wholegrain mustard

1 tbsp white wine vinegar

1 To make dressing, place mayonnaise, stock, mustard and vinegar in a bowl and mix to combine. Set aside.

2 Arrange lettuce, cooked lentils, tomatoes and croutons attractively on a serving platter. Set aside.

3 Heat oil in a skillet over a medium heat, add salmon and cook, turning several times, for 4 minutes or until salmon is cooked. Remove from pan and arrange on top of salad. Drizzle dressing over salad and top with shavings of Parmesan cheese and black pepper to taste.

Serves 4

Roasted Corn and Bean Salad Mexicana

Preparation 12 mins **Cooking** 15 mins **Calories** 188

4 ears of corn

2 red capsicums, chopped

1 green capsicum, chopped

1 red onion, chopped

1 tbsp paprika

1 tbsp ground cumin

2 tbsps oil

2 cloves garlic, ground

6 yellow baby squash

400g (14oz) canned lima beans, rinsed

400g (14oz) canned kidney beans, rinsed

120ml (4 fl oz) vegetable stock

1 tsp Tabasco sauce

1 tsp sugar

juice of 2 limes

¼ cup fresh cilantro, chopped

salt and pepper

1 Cut the corn from the ears and remove and discard the seed core from the capsicums.

2 In a large non-stick pan, add the onion, chopped red and green capsicum flesh, paprika, cumin and the corn and cook over a high heat until the vegetables begin to blacken and blister, stirring often. Remove from the pan and set aside.

3 Add the oil, garlic and squash to the used pan and cook for 4 minutes, stirring constantly.

4 Add the lima beans, kidney beans, stock, Tabasco and sugar and cook until the liquid has evaporated and the vegetables are hot.

5 Remove from the heat and add lime juice, fresh cilantro and salt and pepper to taste. Add the corn mixture and toss thoroughly to coat all the vegetables.

6 Serve warm or at room temperature.

Serves 6–8

Tortilla Salad Mexicana

Preparation 20 mins **Cooking** 5 mins **Calories**

Dressing

1 small mango, peeled,
pitted and diced

½ cup grapefruit juice

¼ cup fresh lime juice

1–2 small red chilies

4 shallots, chopped

2 tbsp vegetable oil

1 clove garlic

Salad

oil for frying

4 corn tortillas, cut into strips

3 cups thinly sliced green
cabbage

3 cups thinly sliced iceberg
lettuce

1 mango, peeled and
flesh diced

1 cup diced, peeled daikon
(white radish)

1 red onion,
finely diced

3 red capsicums, roasted,
peeled and sliced

½ cup shelled pumpkin
seeds, toasted

½ bunch cilantro, chopped

salt and pepper

1 To make the dressing, place all the ingredients in a blender and blend until smooth. Set aside.

2 Next, make the salad. Heat oil in a heavy medium saucepan over medium-high heat.

3 Add a handful of tortilla strips and cook until crisp, about 4 minutes per batch, then remove from the oil and drain on absorbent paper.

4 Combine cabbage, lettuce, mango, daikon, onion, capsicums, pumpkin seeds and cilantro in a large bowl. Toss with enough dressing to coat, adding salt and pepper to taste. Add the tortilla and serve.

Serves 4–6

New Mexico Chicken Salad

Preparation 10 mins **Cooking** None **Calories** 515

1 bunch young arugula

edible flowers of your choice

6 radicchio leaves, shredded

1 grapefruit, peeled, all white pith removed, segmented

2 smoked chicken breasts, sliced

Pine Nut and Chili Dressing

4 tbsps pine nuts, toasted

6 bay leaves

2 fresh red chilies, finely chopped

2 tbsps sugar

⅓ cup red wine vinegar

¼ cup olive oil

1 Arrange arugula, flowers and radicchio attractively on serving plates. Top with grapefruit and chicken.

2 To make dressing, place pine nuts, bay leaves, chilies, sugar, vinegar and oil in a bowl and beat to combine. Just prior to serving, drizzle dressing over salad.

Serves 4

Note: Orange and ½ cup of chopped semi-dried tomatoes can be used instead of grapefruit in this salad.

Squash with Scallions

Preparation 15 mins **Cooking** 30 mins **Calories** 316

1kg (2¼lb) butternut squash, peeled and chopped

340g (12oz) yellow or green baby squash

4 carrots, peeled and halved

zest of 2 limes

1 tbsp olive oil

freshly ground black pepper

150g (5oz) feta cheese, crumbled

Scallion Dressing

12 scallions, sliced

3 mild fresh green chilies, sliced

⅓ cup olive oil

¼ cup cider vinegar

2 tbsps lime juice

1 Preheat oven to 180°C (350°F). Place squash, carrots, lime zest, olive oil and black pepper in a baking dish, toss to combine and bake for 30 minutes or until vegetables are golden and soft.

2 To make dressing, place scallions, chilies, olive oil, vinegar and lime juice in a bowl and beat to combine.

3 Place vegetables on a serving platter, scatter with feta cheese and drizzle with dressing.

Serves 6

Armenian Stuffed Tomato Salad

Preparation 20 mins **Cooking** 20 mins **Calories** 408

8 large, round tomatoes
4 tbsps olive oil
1 large onion, finely chopped
1 large leek, green part removed and finely chopped
3 cups steamed or boiled white or brown rice
½ cup toasted pine nuts
¾ cup dried currants
½ cup parsley, chopped
1 tbsp fresh mint, chopped
¾ tsp sea salt
½ tsp black pepper
2 cloves garlic, crushed
½ cup vegetable stock
½ cup white wine
500g (18oz) baby spinach leaves

1   With a sharp knife, slice the tops off the tomatoes, and scoop out as much flesh as possible without damaging the exterior of the tomato. Chop the tomato pulp finely.

2   Heat the olive oil and cook the chopped onion and leek until slightly golden. Add the rice, tomato pulp, nuts, currants, parsley, mint, salt and pepper and sauté until the mixture is hot and well flavored.

3   Fill each tomato with the rice mixture and replace the tops of the tomatoes. Combine the garlic, stock and white wine and drizzle around tomatoes.

4   Bake at 180°C (350°) for 15 minutes.

5   Meanwhile, wash and dry the spinach leaves. When the tomatoes have finished cooking, remove them and toss the remaining hot liquid through the spinach, discarding the garlic.

6   Serve a mound of warm spinach on each plate with the tomato perched on top. Drizzle any remaining liquid over and serve.

Serves 8

Israeli Kumquat Chicken Salad with Mixed Wild Rice

Preparation 2 hrs **Cooking** 40 mins **Calories** 141

1kg (2¼ lb) lean chicken, diced

1 tsp each of salt, pepper, paprika, ground cumin and onion powder

500ml (18fl oz) orange juice

¼ cup dry white wine

2 onions, diced

4 tbsps apricot preserve

4 tbsps peach preserve

4 tbsps honey

2 tbsps lemon juice

2 tbsps lime juice

500g (18oz) fresh kumquats, or tinned if unavailable

¼ cup wild rice

½ cup brown rice

1 cup white rice

1 bunch basil, leaves thinly sliced

100g (4oz) toasted, chopped pistachio nuts

1 Place the diced chicken in a plastic bag and add the salt, pepper, paprika, ground cumin and onion powder and seal the bag. Shake vigorously to coat the chicken with the spice mix then thread the spiced chicken pieces onto wooden skewers and place them in a shallow baking dish. Set aside.

2 Meanwhile mix the orange juice, wine, onions, both preserves, honey, lemon and lime juice and kumquats and heat until just about to boil. Pour half this mixture (reserving the remaining mixture) over the chicken skewers and marinate for 2 hours.

3 While the chicken is marinating, prepare the rice. Bring a large pot of salted water to the boil and add the wild rice. Boil for 5 minutes then add the brown rice. Boil these together for a further 10 minutes before adding the white rice and simmering for 15 minutes. Drain thoroughly and keep warm.

4 Heat a broiler pan or barbecue and cook the chicken skewers until cooked through, brushing them with the remaining orange mixture as they cook.

5 Fold the finely sliced fresh basil and chopped pistachio nuts through the rice then serve with the chicken skewers. Drizzle any remaining orange mixture over if desired.

Serves 6–8

Middle Eastern Bean and Artichoke Salad

Preparation 10 mins **Cooking** 12–15 mins **Calories** 270

600g (1¼ lb) green beans

800g (1¾ lb) canned chickpeas

8 preserved artichoke hearts, quartered

1 small red onion, peeled and very finely sliced

1 medium carrot, shredded

½ cup parsley, chopped

½ cup cilantro, chopped

2 tbsps fresh dill

2 tbsps white wine vinegar

3 tbsps olive oil

1 clove garlic, crushed

1 tsp mustard

1 tsp ground cumin

juice of 1 large lemon

salt and pepper

100g (4oz) hazelnuts, toasted and roughly chopped

1 Steam the beans until bright green and crisp-tender (do not overcook), drain well and refresh in cold water, then cut diagonally in half.

2 Place them in a large bowl and add the drained and rinsed chickpeas, quartered artichoke hearts, finely sliced red onion, shredded carrot, parsley, cilantro and dill. Stir to combine thoroughly.

3 In a jug, beat the vinegar, olive oil, garlic, mustard, cumin, lemon juice, salt and pepper. When emulsified, pour over the vegetable mixture and toss very well to coat the vegetables in the dressing.

4 Sprinkle with toasted hazelnuts and serve.

Serves 6–8

Turkish Tabouleh

Preparation 40 mins **Cooking** 1 hr **Calories** 101

¾ cup fine bulgur wheat

½ bunch scallions, trimmed and finely sliced

1 large ripe tomato, deseeded and diced

½ red capsicum, deseeded and diced

1 small cucumber, peeled, deseeded and diced

1 cup parsley, finely chopped

¼ cup fresh mint, sliced

2 tbsps red capsicum paste

juice of 1 lemon

3 tbsps olive oil

½ tbsp pomegranate molasses

2 tsps ground cumin

salt and pepper

Turkish Red Capsicum Paste

2 red capsicums, flesh only

2 hot red chilies

½ tsp salt

½ tsp sugar

10ml olive oil

1　To make the Turkish red capsicum paste, place the capsicums, chilies, salt, sugar and olive oil in a blender with 20ml (2 tbsp) water and process until smooth. Transfer the mixture to a saucepan and simmer gently until the mixture is thick and the liquid has reduced, about 1 hour, stirring frequently. Cool.

2　Cover the bulgur with cool water and allow to stand for 30 minutes. Drain well, squeezing out any excess water. In a mixing bowl, combine the bulgur, scallions, tomato, capsicum, cucumber, parsley and mint and mix well. Add the red capsicum paste and mix thoroughly until the salad takes on a lovely red hue.

3　Beat together the lemon juice, olive oil, pomegranate molasses, cumin, salt and pepper. Pour the dressing over the vegetable mixture and toss thoroughly to make sure all the ingredients are coated. Add extra salt to taste, if necessary, then chill for 2 hours. Serve cold or at room temperature.

Serves 4

Moroccan Vegetable Salad

Preparation 2–3 hrs **Cooking** 1 hr **Calories** 538

10 baby onions, peeled
10 cloves garlic, peeled
3 carrots, cut into 5cm (2in) lengths
1 bulb fennel, cut into wedges
4 parsnips, cut into quarters, lengthways
500g (18oz) sweet potatoes, cut into 2cm (1in) thick rounds

Spicy Lime Marinade
1 tsp ground turmeric
1 tsp ground cumin
1 tsp ground cinnamon
½ tsp harissa
2 cloves garlic, crushed
½ cup olive oil
3 tbsps lime juice
1 tbsp honey

Herbed Yogurt
1 cup natural yogurt
2 tbsps fresh dill, chopped
2 tbsps fresh mint, chopped
freshly ground black pepper

1 To make marinade, place turmeric, cumin, cinnamon, harissa, garlic, oil, lime juice and honey in a glass or ceramic bowl and blend to combine.

2 Add onions, garlic, carrots, fennel, parsnips and sweet potatoes to marinade and toss to coat. Cover and marinate in the refrigerator for 2–3 hours.

3 To make herbed yogurt, place yogurt, dill, mint and black pepper to taste in a bowl and mix to combine. Cover and refrigerate until required.

4 Transfer vegetables and marinade to a baking dish and bake for 1 hour or until vegetables are tender. Serve hot or warm with herbed yogurt.

Serves 4

Note: Harissa is a hot chili paste used in North African cooking. It is available from speciality food shops or you can make a simple version yourself by combining 2 tbsps each of chili powder, ground cumin, tomato paste and olive oil with 1 tsp salt.

Marsala Quail Salad

Preparation 10 mins **Cooking** 30 mins **Calories** 444

6 quail
30g (1oz) butter
¾ cup dry Marsala
2 curly endives, leaves separated
1 radicchio, leaves separated
1 bunch watercress
1 pear, peeled, cored and sliced
50g (2oz) pecans

Marsala Sauce
½ cup cream
2 tbsps mayonnaise
2 tsps dry Marsala

1 Place quail on a rack in a ovenproof dish and bake for 20 minutes. Cool slightly, then break into serving-size portions.

2 Melt butter in a saucepan. Add cream and Marsala, bring to the boil, then reduce heat and simmer for 5 minutes. Add quail and cook for 5 minutes longer. Set aside to cool.

3 To make sauce, combine cream, mayonnaise and Marsala and beat well to combine.

4 Arrange endive, radicchio, watercress and pear in a serving bowl. Top with quail, sprinkle with pecans and drizzle sauce over. Serve immediately.

Serves 6

Indian Chickpea Salad with Spinach

Preparation 2 hrs **Cooking** 30 mins **Calories** 170

2 cups dry chickpeas
4 onions
1 tsp whole cloves
4 bay leaves
60ml (4 tbsp) peanut or olive oil
4 cloves garlic, crushed
1 tsp ground turmeric
2 tsps ground cumin
2 tsps garam masala
3 tbsps tomato paste
2 red capsicums, sliced
4 medium zucchini, sliced on the diagonal
salt and pepper
500g (18oz) baby spinach

1 Pick over the chickpeas and remove any that are discolored. Place all remaining chickpeas in a large saucepan and cover with cold water. Peel 2 of the onions and chop in half. Place these in the saucepan with the chickpeas. Add the cloves and bay leaves and bring to the boil and simmer for 10 minutes then remove the chickpeas from the heat and cover and allow to steep for 2 hours. Strain the chickpeas, discarding the onions, cloves and bay leaves, reserving some of the soaking water.

2 Meanwhile, chop the remaining 2 onions. Heat the oil and sauté the onions and the crushed garlic. Add all the spices and cook briefly to release their fragrance. Add the soaked chickpeas and 2 cups of the soaking water, the tomato paste and the red capsicum strips.

3 Cover and simmer gently for about 20 minutes until the chickpeas soften and the liquid evaporates. Add the zucchini and salt and pepper to taste and stir well then remove from the heat. Allow to cool slightly then fold through the spinach leaves. Cool completely and serve.

Serves 8

Note: Never add salt to pulses until after the initial cooking or soaking because the salt will toughen the skin of the bean and inhibit its ability to absorb liquid.

Indian Salad of Spiced Chicken and Dhal

Preparation 15 mins **Cooking** 35 mins **Calories** 559

7½ cups vegetable stock
1½ cups dried lentils
juice of 2 lemons
2 tbsp vegetable oil
1 tbsp curry powder
1 tbsp garam masala
1 tsp turmeric
salt and pepper
4 large chicken breast fillets, skin removed
1 small cauliflower, cut into florets
1½ cups fresh or frozen peas
2 small tomatoes, deseeded and diced
1 cucumber, peeled and diced
2 scallions, sliced
2 tbsps fresh mint, chopped
2 large bunches watercress, trimmed

1 Bring 6 cups of vegetable stock to the boil and add the lentils. Simmer until the lentils are tender, but still retain their shape, about 20 minutes. Drain well then transfer the lentils to a large bowl and add the lemon juice and 1 tbsp of the oil. Mix well, cover and chill.

2 Combine the curry powder, garam masala and turmeric in a plastic bag with salt and pepper to taste then add the chicken breasts to the bag. Seal the bag and shake vigorously, allowing the spices to coat the chicken breasts evenly. Heat a non-stick skillet with the remaining oil until smoking then add the chicken breasts to the pan until golden brown and cooked through on both sides, about 5 minutes. Remove the chicken and set aside.

3 To the used pan, add the remaining stock and bring to the boil. Add the cauliflower and peas and cook over high heat until vegetables are crisp-tender and most of liquid has evaporated, about 5 minutes. Add this vegetable mixture to the lentils and mix well. Add the diced tomatoes, diced cucumber, sliced scallions and chopped fresh mint and mix well, adding more salt and pepper to taste.

4 Slice the chicken into diagonal strips then gently mix these into the salad. Arrange the watercress on a platter and top with the salad mixture, arranging so that there is plenty of chicken visible. Garnish with extra mint.

Serves 6–8

Pakistani Green Bean Salad with Cilantro and Ginger

Preparation 10 mins **Cooking** 15 mins **Calories** 94

700g (1¾lb) fresh snap beans
2cm (1in) piece fresh ginger
1 tbsp vegetable oil
1 tbsp sesame oil
1 tsp mustard seeds
2 tsps ground cumin
½ tsp ground turmeric
1 fresh green chili, finely minced
150ml (5fl oz) chicken or vegetable stock
juice of 2 lemons
1 bunch fresh cilantro, washed, dried then chopped
salt
80g (3oz) peanuts, roasted and chopped

1 Trim the beans to lengths of 8cm (2in) and discard any discolored ends. Peel the ginger and cut into fine matchstalks.

2 Heat a wok with the vegetable and sesame oils and, when hot, add the mustard seeds. Allow them to cook for a moment or two until they start popping. Add the ginger and cook for a further minute. Add the ground cumin, turmeric and chili and stir until fragrant, about 2 minutes.

3 Add all the beans and toss in the flavored oil to coat them thoroughly. Add the stock, cover and simmer for 5–8 minutes or until the liquid has almost evaporated completely and the beans are tender.

4 Remove the lid and add the lemon juice, cilantro and salt to taste. Stir thoroughly to combine all the ingredients then cool. Serve garnished with roasted chopped peanuts and, if desired, lemon wedges.

Serves 4–6

Tandoori Lamb with Black Onion Seeds, Sesame and Salad

Preparation 4 hrs **Cooking** 10 mins **Calories** 508

12 large lamb cutlets
1 cup sesame seeds
½ cup black onion seeds

Marinade
1 large onion, chopped
20g (1oz) piece fresh ginger, shredded
juice of 1 lemon
½ cup plain yogurt
2 tsps ground cilantro
2 tsps ground cumin
½ tsp ground turmeric
¼ tsp cayenne pepper
1 tbsp garam masala
¼ tsp mace
1 tsp salt

Salad
250g (9oz) baby spinach leaves
200g (7oz) mixed baby lettuce leaves
4 scallions, sliced
2 tbsp white vinegar
4 tbsp peanut oil
salt and pepper
few drops toasted sesame oil

1 Place the onion, ginger, lemon juice and 1 tbsp water in a blender with the yogurt, spices and salt and process until the mixture is smooth. Remove from the blender and pour over the lamb cutlets, turning to coat both sides of the lamb. Marinate for a minimum of 4 hours or up to 8 hours.

2 Preheat the oven to 220°C (425°F). When you are ready to cook, mix the sesame seeds and onion seeds together and place them on a plate. Remove the lamb cutlets from the marinade one at a time, allowing the excess marinade to run off, then dip each cutlet in the sesame mixture, coating both sides. Place the coated cutlets on a non-stick baking sheet and bake in the preheated oven for 10 minutes for medium rare, or longer if you prefer.

3 Meanwhile, prepare the salad. Wash and dry the spinach and mixed lettuce leaves and place them, with the scallions, in a large salad bowl. Beat together the vinegar and peanut oil with salt and pepper to taste then add the few drops of sesame oil, continuing to beat until the dressing is thick. Toss the salad with the dressing until the leaves are well coated then divide the salad between 6 plates. Arrange 2 cutlets on each plate and serve immediately.

Serves 6

Note: Black onion seeds (nigella) are available from Indian grocery stores. If unavailable, simply use extra sesame seeds.

Index